LAUREL COUNTY PUBLIC LIBRARY

Why did
WORLD WAR II
happen?

CATH SENKER

Gareth Stevens
Publishing

Please visit our Web site, www.garethstevens.com.
For a free color catalog of all our high-quality books,
call toll free 1-800-542-2595 or fax 1-877-542-2596.

Library of Congress Cataloging-in-Publication Data

Senker, Cath.
 Why did World War II happen? / Cath Senker.
   p. cm. -- (Moments in history)
 Includes index.
 ISBN 978-1-4339-4184-9 (library binding)
 ISBN 978-1-4339-4185-6 (pbk.)
 ISBN 978-1-4339-4186-3 (6-pack)
 1. World War, 1939-1945--Juvenile literature. I. Title.
 II. Title: Why did World War Two happen? III. Title:
 Why did World War 2 happen?
 D743.7.S35 2011
 940.53--dc22
                      2010015834

First Edition

Published in 2011 by
Gareth Stevens Publishing
111 East 14th Street, Suite 349
New York, NY 10003

Copyright © 2011 Arcturus Publishing

Series concept: Alex Woolf
Editors: Philip de Ste. Croix and Honor Head
Designer: Andrew Easton
Picture researcher: Thomas Mitchell
Maps: Encompass Graphics
Project manager: Joe Harris

Photo credits: All the photographs in this book were
supplied by Getty Images, except for cover image:
Hulton-Deutsch Collection/CORBIS. Pages 17, 24, 25,
30, 43 Time Life Pictures/Getty Images.
All rights reserved. No part of this book may be
reproduced in any form without permission in writing
from the publisher, except by a reviewer.

Printed in the United States of America

CPSIA compliance information: Batch #AS10GS: For further information contact
Gareth Stevens, New York, New York at 1-800-542-2595.

SL001517US

CONTENTS

CHAPTER 1

THE GATHERING STORM

The seeds of the twentieth century's second great global conflict were sown in the bitter aftermath of its first. However, World War II surpassed World War I in scale—this devastating conflict drew in 61 countries, which represented three-quarters of the world's population. The vast death toll included about 25 million military personnel and 25 million civilians. Millions more were left wounded and homeless.

There were three main areas of conflict: Europe, the Far East, and the Pacific Ocean. The European war spread to North Africa, and Southeast Asia became involved in the Far East conflict. The war was fought on land in four major campaigns, at sea (in the Mediterranean, the Atlantic, and the Pacific), and in the skies above the conflict zones.

GERMANY HUMILIATED IN DEFEAT

Some of the causes of World War II can be found in the terms of the Treaty of Versailles of 1919. After World War I, the Allies, led by France, Britain, and the United States, forced Germany to sign the treaty, which left many Germans feeling humiliated and aggrieved. Under the terms of

The German economy collapsed in 1923 as a result of the massive war debts and reparations that Germany had to pay after World War II. Inflation in Germany was out of control and its currency became worthless. It was common for many Germans to exchange goods and services for food.

A cavalry patrol under the command of Chinese general Chiang Kai-shek rides through Canton, China, in 1925. In 1928, Chiang Kai-shek established a national government, which was opposed by the Communist forces in the country.

settlement, Germany lost territory to France, Belgium, Denmark, and Poland, and the coal-rich Saar region was taken over by the League of Nations. The treaty also forced Germany to disarm its military forces and pay reparations for having started the war to the victorious countries. In 1921, the amount was fixed at 132 billion gold marks—an enormous sum.

Germany was also in political turmoil during the postwar years. In 1918, its first democratic government, known as the Weimar Republic, was established. However, this government was weak and was threatened by both left-wing and right-wing groups. In 1919, a rebellion broke out known

VOICES FROM HISTORY

Fury in defeat

This extract from the newspaper the *Deutsche Zeitung*, in 1919, clearly demonstrates how angry the German people felt at what they saw as the unfair demands of the Treaty of Versailles:

"Today in … Versailles the disgraceful Treaty is being signed. Do not forget it! The German people will with unceasing labour press forward to reconquer the place among nations to which it is entitled. Then will come vengeance for the shame of 1919."

Quoted in Stewart Ross, *The Causes and Consequences of the Second World War* (Evans Brothers, 2003)

Japanese soldiers entering Manchuria in China. In September 1931, Japan began its takeover of Manchuria by attacking the Chinese garrison in Mukden. Within a few months, the takeover was complete and Manchuria was renamed Manchukuo.

as the Spartacist Rising, during which left-wing Communists seized Berlin and other German cities. But the government managed to defeat them. Then, in 1920, the right-wing anticommunist Freikorps attempted to take power during a coup. The Weimar Republic survived this threat but was left even more undermined.

In the Far East, conflict was brewing between Japan and China. Japan's government was heavily influenced by military leaders who were determined to win control over neighboring east Asian countries, including China. Since 1928, the Chinese government had been struggling against the Communists, who wanted to take over the country. Japan planned to take advantage of the instability in China to conquer Chinese territory.

THE LEAGUE OF NATIONS

As part of the peace settlement of 1919, an international organization, the League of Nations, had been established to try to prevent aggression between countries, such as the Japanese threat to China, from leading to war. The organization adopted the principle of collective security. This meant that member countries agreed to act together against an aggressor to prevent international disputes from leading to war. They could do this collectively using peaceful means, such as economic sanctions or diplomatic talks.

The League of Nations was supposed

VOICES FROM HISTORY

Bread lines and soup kitchens

During the Great Depression, millions of people across America lost their money and their jobs, and found themselves on the poverty line. Carmen Carter, who wrote this excerpt, could count herself lucky:

"In 1929 Orlo and I had been married two years and had a year-old son, Douglas. We were just nicely getting started in the turkey raising business on his parents' farm near Bridgeton. … But that year was different. The newspapers were full of news about banks closing, businesses failing, and people out of work. There was just no money and we could not sell the turkeys. So we were in debt with no way out. … But when we read about the bread lines and soup kitchens in the cities, we felt we were lucky because we raised our own food."

Carmen Carter, *Michigan History Magazine*, January–February 1982 (Vol. 66, No. 1)

conquer territory in China, and overran the Chinese province of Manchuria. Again, the League did nothing.

Economic hardship was also causing worldwide problems. In 1929, the Great Depression, a dramatic economic collapse, hit the United States. Industrial production declined, many factories closed, and millions of workers lost their jobs. Short of money, the United States took back huge sums that it had loaned to other countries, such as Britain and Germany. There was a massive decline in international trade because the United States could no longer afford to buy large quantities of goods from other countries. This affected production in those places, and the Depression spread around the world. Between 1929 and the end of 1933, industrial production worldwide shrank

Bewildered and angry, workers pour onto the streets of New York City on October 29, 1929. Following the collapse in share prices in New York—known as the Great Crash—the savings of many thousands of people became worthless overnight. The stock market did not recover and the U.S. economy went into deep depression.

to represent all the countries of the world, but many powerful nations were not members—Germany was not allowed to join until 1926, the United States declined to become a member, and the Soviet Union (USSR) did not join until 1934. Japan and Germany left the League in 1933, and Italy left in 1937. Moreover, the League had no military force of its own. In 1923, Italy attacked the Greek island of Corfu, but the League took no action. In 1931, Japan began to carry out its plan to

by a massive 40 percent.

These serious economic problems worsened the political divisions in Europe, especially in unstable countries such as Germany and Spain. As unemployment and poverty increased, many people no longer trusted their governments. Disillusioned, people were ready to try a different type of government. There was a dramatic rise in the popularity of Communism and other left-wing groups, as well as interest in extreme right-wing political parties.

In Spain and Germany, support grew for fascism (Italy had had a fascist government since 1922). The fascists believed in rule by one strong leader and thought that their nation was superior to others. They were prepared to use force against enemies in their country and to conquer other nations. Germany's fascist party, the Nazi Party, argued that Jewish people were to blame for the country's problems.

Fascism was becoming a dangerous threat to world peace. In 1933, the Nazi Party came to power in Germany. The Nazi leader, Adolf Hitler, promised to seize back German territory lost under the Treaty of Versailles and conquer new lands to make Germany a great power. Italy's fascist government, led by Benito Mussolini, also wanted to expand Italy's borders. Having captured Corfu in 1923, Mussolini attacked Abyssinia (modern-day Ethiopia) in 1935.

Against the backdrop of increasing conflict around the world, European nations rearmed in the belief that war was coming. In 1936, Germany, Britain, and France began serious rearmament.

Adolf Hitler addresses a huge rally of storm troopers in Dortmund in 1933. Storm troopers were an armed group formed by Hitler that used violence to crush any opposition to the Nazis. These rallies showed the strength of the Nazi Party and attracted many people to its cause.

Hitler takes control

Germany had an electoral system known as proportional representation. This meant that at elections each party gained seats in the Reichstag (parliament) in proportion to the number of votes it received. Political parties that held similar policies could create a coalition to form the government. In the November 1932 elections, the Nazis won 196 seats and the Communists won 100. The moderate left-wing SPD (Social Democrats) won 121 seats. If the Communists and SPD had formed a coalition, they would have had more seats than the Nazis and could have established a government, and history might have been very different. But the largest party was the Nazi Party, and in January 1933, President Paul von Hindenburg appointed Hitler, the party's leader, chancellor of Germany— making war more likely.

According to the Treaty of Versailles, Germany was only permitted a small army and was not allowed to have an air force, submarines, or large battleships. But Germany rearmed secretly. In 1936, Britain started to develop new fighter aircraft, and conscription was introduced in early 1939. France increased its military expenditure tenfold between 1934 and 1939.

German troops and tanks parade through Vienna, the capital city of Austria. When Germany occupied Austria in 1938, there was no fighting; many Austrians welcomed the prospect of being united with Germany.

WAR IN ASIA

While Europe was busy preparing for war, conflict erupted in east Asia. In 1937, war broke out between Japan and China. Japan seized the major Chinese cities of Tianjin, Beijing, Nanking, and Shanghai. It soon became clear that Japan planned to acquire other territories in Southeast Asia. This would potentially draw European countries into the dispute, as Britain and France had colonies in the region that would be threatened by Japanese expansion. The United States also had commercial and strategic interests in east Asia.

Meanwhile, in Europe, Hitler began his campaign to expand Germany's territory. In 1936, his troops reoccupied the Rhineland on the border with France. This area had been declared a demilitarized zone by the Treaty

British prime minister Neville Chamberlain (left) with Adolf Hitler in Munich in September 1938. The French prime minister, Edouard Daladier, also flew to Germany to sign the Munich Agreement. There were high hopes among both the French and British that the new agreement would prevent war and "ensure peace in our time."

appeasement in response to Hitler's actions. In 1938, British prime minister Neville Chamberlain accepted Hitler's annexation of Austria. Then he met Hitler in September 1938 at a conference in Munich, Germany, to discuss the future of Czechoslovakia in the face of Hitler's territorial demands. This resulted in the Munich Agreement, which was signed by Nazi Germany, Britain, France, and Italy. Under its terms, it was agreed that Czechoslovakia had to give up the Sudetenland to Germany, although no one had consulted the Czechs about giving up their land. Again, Chamberlain hoped that giving in to Hitler's demands in the Sudetenland would stop him from making further territorial claims that might lead to war. At the meeting, Hitler agreed that the Sudetenland was his final European land claim. However, he had no intention of changing his aim of expanding Germany's borders.

War Is Declared

In March 1939, Nazi forces occupied the whole of Czechoslovakia, and Hitler drew up plans to attack Poland. In May, Hitler secured a full political and military alliance with Italy, called the Pact of Steel. Then, in August, he signed a nonaggression pact with the Soviet Union, under which the two countries agreed not to attack each other, nor to support any other country that might attack one of them.

Both the USSR and Germany knew that in reality this pact was merely a temporary measure to postpone war between them. It made sense to Hitler because it meant he could attack

of Versailles, but the international community said and did nothing. Emboldened by success, in March 1938, Hitler incorporated Austria into Germany, again in defiance of the Treaty of Versailles. He then claimed that the Sudetenland region in western Czechoslovakia should be handed over to Germany because more than 3 million German-speaking citizens lived there.

Since the early 1930s, in the hope of avoiding a war, the British government had pursued a policy of

WHY DID IT HAPPEN

Who started World War II?

Until the 1960s, most historians were in agreement that Hitler meant to start a world war. Then, in 1961, British historian A. J. P. Taylor claimed that Hitler had intended a series of much smaller conflicts in order to make territorial gains. However, after studying German documents at length, U.S. history professor Gerhard Weinberg concluded that Hitler had indeed been determined to go to war "and hoped to conquer the entire world."

A. J. P. Taylor, *The Second World War* (Hamish Hamilton, 1975); Gerhard Weinberg, *The Foreign Policy of Hitler's Germany* (Humanities Press International, 1994)

Poland, which bordered the USSR, without the intervention of the Soviet Union. It was useful to the USSR, too, because the country was unprepared for war, and because it had its own plans to take over Polish territory.

In August, Hitler made his move on Poland. He announced that he wanted to take over the Polish city of Danzig in the Baltic. Britain, Poland's ally, and France tried to persuade Poland to accept Hitler's demands, but the Polish government refused. On September 1, 1939, Hitler invaded Poland. He thought the Western powers would not intervene, but this time he was wrong. The Allied countries, Britain and France, declared war on Germany.

German soldiers advance along a country road in Poland during the invasion of September 1, 1939. The German tanks met little resistance, since bombers had made a devastating attack on Polish communication lines and military strongpoints.

CHAPTER 2

EUROPE GOES TO WAR

Although Britain and France had declared war on Germany, it was several months before armed conflict began. Britain and France believed that little would be gained by an attack on Germany, and that the German economy was already stretched to the breaking point and likely to collapse. But both Britain and France set up war governments, with ministries of information, and an Allied Supreme Council was established to coordinate policies between the two countries. This period became known as "the phoney war."

While Britain and France hesitated, in spring 1940 Hitler moved

quickly, beginning the Blitzkrieg—"lightning war." In April, German troops occupied Denmark. In May, the German army invaded Holland, Belgium, and Luxembourg. The Dutch were defeated within five days. Belgium and Luxembourg also fell quickly. By June, Norway had also fallen to the Nazis.

In May 1940, the Germans also attacked France and met only feeble

The Nazi invasions of 1939 to 1941. As well as advancing through Europe and into the Soviet Union, in 1941 German forces also joined the Italians in their invasions of North Africa that had begun in 1940.

resistance. Winston Churchill, the new British prime minister, promised to send military aid to the French. However, the British Expeditionary Force faced defeat by the Germans and its commander, General John Gort, decided to retreat rather than suffer enormous losses in France. He successfully evacuated his troops from Dunkirk, a remarkable accomplishment for the British but an action that left the French angry at being deserted by their ally. French soldiers who were left behind were captured by the Germans and taken as prisoners of war.

By June 1940, the Nazis had control of France. Hitler's plan was to divide up the country. Northern France and the entire coast down to the border with Spain would remain occupied by the Nazis, while France south of the Loire River would be ruled by a French government based at Vichy. This government, led by Marshal

VOICES FROM HISTORY

"Blood, toil, tears, and sweat"

On May 10, 1940, Winston Churchill became the British prime minister. Three days later, he made a stirring speech to Parliament opposing the appeasement policy:

"I have nothing to offer but blood, toil, tears and sweat. ... You ask, what is our policy? I will say: It is to wage war, by sea, land and air, with all our might and with all the strength that God can give us. ... You ask, What is our aim? I can answer in one word: Victory—victory at all costs, victory in spite of all terror; victory, however long and hard the road may be."

Quoted in A. J. P. Taylor, *The Second World War* (Hamish Hamilton, 1975)

Between May 26 and June 4, 1940, thousands of troops of the British Expeditionary Force were rescued from the beaches at Dunkirk, northern France.

Philippe Pétain, was controlled by the Nazis—every official measure needed Nazi approval. In a little less than a year, Hitler had gained control of nearly all of Europe west of Soviet Russia. At this point, Italy's fascist leader, Benito Mussolini, declared war on the Allies and joined the conflict on Germany's side.

A British Hurricane fighter plane is refueled during the Battle of Britain in August 1940. The RAF had several advantages over the Germans. They not only had radar that could identify the position of Luftwaffe aircraft, but the British air force was also operating over home territory and could attack, land, and refuel relatively easily.

THE BATTLE OF BRITAIN

Hitler hoped that Britain would make peace with Germany because he knew it would be a difficult country to defeat. Not only was it a well-protected island, it was also a power in the Mediterranean—fighting Britain would mean sending German forces to North Africa. But Churchill would not consider peace with Germany, so Hitler prepared for war. Hitler knew that the German navy was far smaller than Britain's, so rather than risk a conflict at sea, he

decided to bomb Britain's air defenses in preparation for invasion. From July to October 1940, the German air force, the Luftwaffe, bombed British military targets such as harbors and airfields, as well as factories and surrounding houses, in an attempt to disrupt military production. This became known as the Battle of Britain. In early September, it looked as though the Germans were succeeding in wearing down Britain's defenses.

However, Britain had developed a radar system that warned Royal Air Force fighter pilots when bombers were

TURNING POINTS IN HISTORY

Britain commands the skies

During the Battle of Britain, British Fighter Command had just enough aircraft to keep up the fight against the German Luftwaffe. This was achieved by the continual manufacture of new planes and the speedy repair of damaged ones. In contrast, the Luftwaffe did not have enough fighter planes to escort its bombers on their missions from Germany, give them cover, and also to engage the British fighters. The Germans badly underestimated the strength of the RAF. Their failure in the Battle of Britain was a turning point in their war. Without command of the skies, Germany could not successfully invade Britain.

approaching so they could intercept them before they reached their chosen targets. Britain's Hurricane and Spitfire fighter aircraft were able to destroy the German bombers. Between August 12 and the end of September, the Luftwaffe lost over 1,773 aircraft while Britain lost 915. Hitler then postponed his planned invasion of Britain indefinitely.

THE BLITZ BEGINS

After the failure of the Battle of Britain, Germany changed tactics and began to bomb British cities at night, a campaign that became known as the Blitz. Between September 1940 and May 1941, German bombers attacked railways, ports, and city centers in an attempt to disrupt communications, cause chaos, and destroy morale. About 3.5 million homes were damaged or demolished, and around 43,000 people were killed. However, the often indiscriminate

Firefighters in the city of London put out a fire on December 30, 1940. Bombing raids during the Blitz caused huge fires all over London and other British cities. Firefighters often had to blow up buildings to create firebreaks to stop the fires from spreading.

A German U-boat surfaces in 1940. These infamous submarines often traveled and attacked in packs. They were able to target British ships with deadly accuracy, as German code breakers had worked out how to read British naval signals.

the Battle of the Atlantic, Germany used its U-boats (submarines) to attack British shipping in the Atlantic Ocean. Between June and December 1940, U-boats sank over 3 million tons of Allied shipping, which meant a huge reduction in the amount of supplies reaching Britain. Food rationing had already been introduced in the country in January 1940, and in spring 1941 rations were reduced still further.

In order to prevent any additional serious losses at sea, British vessels started to travel in convoys. The RAF patrolled the sea lanes to protect the vessels from attack. The United States sent warships to patrol the western Atlantic. By autumn 1941, these warships were also sinking U-boats.

AXIS POWERS JOIN FORCES

During the Battle of the Atlantic, Hitler shored up Germany's position by forging a series of alliances. He initiated a Tripartite Pact between Japan, Italy, and Germany, which was signed in September 1940. Under the terms of this pact, each country promised to enter into the war if any of the others was attacked by a new enemy. They became known as the Axis Powers.

The Italian leader, Mussolini, had not been involved in Hitler's war plan up to this point. Mussolini had his own ambitions: he wanted to expand Italy's

bombing did not seriously affect war production.

Britain, in return, also conducted a bombing campaign over Germany. The British air force did not have enough fighter planes to provide cover for the daytime bombing of key industries, so the British embarked on the indiscriminate nighttime bombing of German cities. This campaign ended in November 1941 when the Royal Air Force realized its bombing strategy was more costly to Britain in terms of air crew and production than it was to Germany.

After the failure of the Blitz campaign, Hitler adopted a new tactic against Britain in June 1940—blockade. In a campaign that became known as

TURNING POINTS IN HISTORY

Cracking the Enigma codes

The complexity of Germany's Enigma code system was a great challenge to British code breakers. The first breakthrough came in 1940, when British intelligence succeeded in deciphering some of the codes. In May 1941, the British Royal Navy captured a German submarine with its Enigma machine and code books. From then on, the Allies could decode naval messages, which made a major contribution to their intelligence operations during the Battle of the Atlantic.

territory in Africa. In August 1940, Mussolini sent troops into Somaliland (modern Somalia and Djibouti), and the following month an Italian force entered Egypt. In October, Italian forces launched an attack on Greece and on Tobruk, in northeastern Libya.

Britain maintained a naval fleet in the Mediterranean, and had an army in Egypt to protect the Suez Canal, a key element in the shipping route to its empire. The British navy attacked Italian ships at Taranto, Italy, in November and recaptured the port of Tobruk the following January. The Italian offensive was a complete failure.

In March 1941, the United States set

German soldiers use an Enigma enciphering machine to compose a coded message. The use of coded messages had become an essential part of warfare. The Germans used about 200 different Enigma keys, or codes, which were changed every 24 hours.

A convoy of German tanks in Cyrenaica, Libya. A colony belonging to Libya since 1912, Cyrenaica became a major battlefield during World War II. The British occupied the area after the second battle of El Alamein in October 1942.

up a new system to support the Allies by instituting a lend-lease policy. This meant Britain could place orders for American materials, which were paid for by the U.S. government. The materials were leased to Britain, which promised to pay for them after the war. This economic backing gave the United States a powerful role in the war.

The conflict was now spreading further into Europe and the Middle East. In spring 1941, Hitler went to the aid of Italy in its failing campaigns in southeastern Europe. Italy had invaded Greece in October 1940 but had failed to conquer the country. German forces now took control of Greece as well as Crete and Yugoslavia. In addition, the Nazis helped the Italians fight the British forces in North Africa, in an attempt to take control of British colonies there. The conflict soon spread to Syria, Lebanon, and Iraq.

In March 1941, Nazi general Erwin Rommel attacked Tripoli in Libya, and the following month his army entered Egypt. Germany then threatened Syria, a French colony, but was defeated by French forces in June. Then, in late June, the focus of attention moved abruptly away from the Middle East and back to Europe.

HITLER INVADES THE SOVIET UNION

One of Hitler's main aims in the war was to conquer the USSR. His policy of lebensraum (living space) was to provide more land for the German people, and he planned to set up German colonies in areas such as the Ukraine. He also wanted the rich natural resources found there—especially oil. Hitler thought the Soviet Union would be an easy conquest. On June 22, 1941, he launched Operation Barbarossa, the invasion of the Soviet

WHY DID IT HAPPEN ?

Winston Churchill: defender of democracy?

In his argument that Churchill was a "defender of democracy," British historian Professor Geoffrey Best stated that: "The normal peacetime freedoms of the citizen were of course restricted but rarely beyond the limits of reason. The world could see no hypocrisy in Churchill's claim to be fighting for democracy and human rights against tyranny and barbarism."

However, left-wing historian Chris Harman argued that Churchill was a hypocrite because he did not support democracy in other places, especially in British colonies. During the war, Churchill said: "I did not become his majesty's first minister in order to preside over the dissolution of the British Empire." In 1942, the Quit India campaign against British rule in India was crushed by British forces.

Geoffrey Best, "Winston Churchill: Defender of Democracy," BBC History website, 2002; Chris Harman, *A People's History of the World* (Bookmarks, 1999)

Union. This soon became one of the biggest conflicts of the war. Hungary and Romania were drawn into the war on Germany's side, and the USSR sought help from the Allies. Britain offered to support the Soviet Union with nonmilitary supplies, but the USSR had to rely on its own military resources in its fight against Hitler.

German forces advanced on Leningrad in August 1941 and began a siege of the city that lasted 900 days and caused around 800,000 civilian deaths. In September, the Germans captured the Ukraine, most of the Crimea, and the Donets basin. By the end of September, the German advance on the capital, Moscow, had begun. However, they were halted in the winter of 1941–42 by the freezing weather and lack of resources. This was not going to be the quick war Hitler had hoped for.

German soldiers march through a burning Russian village during Operation Barbarossa, the German invasion of the Soviet Union. The invasion began in June 1941. Russia had not armed itself against such an attack, as it feared this might provoke war with Germany.

GLOBAL WAR

Germany and Italy were not the only nations with aggressive territorial ambitions. Japan had plans to carve out its own Asian empire. While the struggle between Germany and the USSR was underway during the second half of 1941, the conflict in east Asia also grew in size and intensity. Japan's threat to Western colonies in the region provoked the Allies to join the war in the Far East that Japan and China had been fighting since 1937.

Japan's rulers believed that the U.S. was so involved with Europe that it would not interfere with Japan's attempts to expand its territory. However, this was not the case. The United States had business and strategic interests in the Pacific that it would fight to protect.

Japanese forces entered the French colony of Indochina in July 1941. In response, the United States imposed an embargo to prevent the supply of oil to Japan. It also froze Japanese assets, which meant that Japanese businesses

U.S. warships ablaze at anchor in Pearl Harbor on Hawaii on December 7, 1941, following an attack by Japanese aircraft. The Americans had received information from intelligence sources and from the Allies that some form of Japanese attack was imminent, but failed to take any action.

British prisoners of war (POWs) being transported from Hong Kong to a Japanese prison camp. The British had not ensured that Hong Kong was properly protected and the island was easily captured by Japanese forces in December 1941. Conditions in Japanese camps were extremely harsh. By the time Japan surrendered in 1945, 27 percent of the POWs from Britain and the Allied countries of the British Commonwealth and 37 percent of American POWs had died in captivity.

TURNING POINTS IN HISTORY

Pearl Harbor targeted

Japan was eager to join Italy and Germany in their fight for new territory. Tojo Hideki, appointed Japanese prime minister in October 1941, believed in the supremacy of the Japanese people and wanted to create an empire in Asia. He knew that the oil embargo against Japan by the U.S. would soon have a serious effect on the Japanese economy, as the country was using nearly ten times as much oil as it could produce per year. Japan would either have to back down or fight the United States. Japanese admiral Yamamoto Isoroku decided that a first strike against its enemy's naval fleet at Pearl Harbor could stop the United States from thwarting Japan's expansion plans. However, the attack on Pearl Harbor was not the spectacular victory that Yamamoto hoped for.

in the United States could no longer operate. U.S. president Franklin D. Roosevelt said these restrictions would be lifted only when Japan pulled its troops out of Indochina and China.

The restrictions didn't succeed in keeping Japan in check. On the contrary, on December 7, Japanese forces went on the offensive with a surprise attack on Pearl Harbor, an important U.S. naval base in Hawaii. They destroyed much of America's naval fleet and 2,403 U.S. troops and 64 Japanese lost their lives. However, Japan failed to destroy America's oil reserves in Hawaii and did not hit any aircraft carriers, which by chance were at sea on that day. However, the attack led Britain and the United States immediately to declare war on Japan. In response, Germany and Italy declared war on the United States.

BATTLES IN THE PACIFIC
To consolidate their position, the Japanese invaded Malaya, Thailand, and the Philippines on the day after the attack on Pearl Harbor, and attacked Burma three days later. On December

21

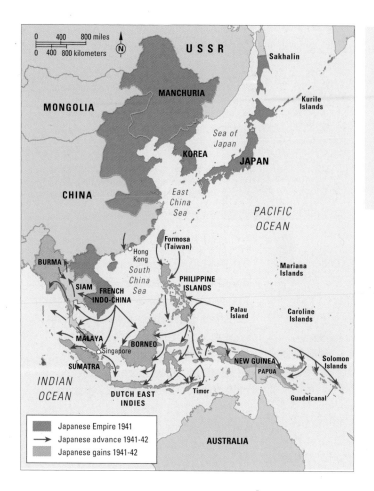

This map shows the extent of the Japanese empire in 1941 and how much it expanded after Japan joined World War II. The Japanese empire was at its greatest in 1942, after which Japanese forces were pushed back toward their homeland as the Allies went on the counteroffensive.

22, they captured Manila, capital of the U.S.-controlled Philippines, from American forces. On Christmas Day, they took Hong Kong (an island near China) from the British—along with 12,000 prisoners of war. Churchill called this "the worst disaster and largest capitulation in British history."

By the end of 1941, Japan, Germany, and Italy had all vastly increased their territory, and they continued their conquests throughout 1942. Over a period of three months, Japan captured long-established colonies from the Western powers. One of these was the Philippines. There, U.S. forces gave up the fight against the Japanese in late February, leaving the Filipinos to continue the resistance. By May, the Philippines had surrendered to Japan.

Encouraged by their success, Japanese forces continued their expansion into Malaya, Singapore, Borneo, Burma, and the Dutch East Indies. By March 1942, the Japanese had conquered a large amount of territory from the borders of India to the borders of Australia, and far out into the Pacific Ocean, including the Solomon, Marshall, and Mariana islands. The Australian government prepared its forces for a possible invasion by Japan.

After March 1942, the United States

won some important victories against Japan, which helped to slow down Japan's advance southward. The United States won the Battle of the Coral Sea (May) and the Battle of Midway (June). It adopted a strategy of "island hopping"—recapturing territory by moving eastward island by island across the Pacific Ocean. In August 1942, U.S. Marines landed on Guadalcanal, one of the largest of the Solomon Islands. After a six-month struggle, the island was eventually won by the Americans in February 1943.

In July 1942, the Japanese had

American aircraft carrier USS *Yorktown* under attack during the Battle of Midway in June 1942. This was the first decisive defeat that Japan suffered at the hands of U.S. forces. USS *Yorktown* was the only aircraft carrier that was lost to the U.S. The Japanese lost four.

TURNING POINTS IN HISTORY

Battle of Midway

Japanese admiral Yamamoto Isoroku planned an attack of the U.S.-held islands of Midway to use them as a base from which to attack Hawaii and the Pacific coast of America. What he didn't realize was that the United States had intercepted Japanese naval codes and knew about the plan. The Japanese navy underestimated the U.S. forces on Midway. Within twenty-four hours, Japan lost all four of its largest aircraft carriers, 332 aircraft, and 3,500 sailors. This was a huge loss for Japan.

"

VOICES FROM HISTORY

Montgomery defended

The British commander in chief in the Middle East, Harold Alexander, worked closely with General Montgomery at the Second Battle of El Alamein. In his autobiography, he defended Montgomery's actions in not completely destroying Rommel's army.

"At Alamein Rommel was utterly defeated but not annihilated: Alamein was a decisive victory but not a complete one. It is easy to look back after eighteen years and suggest that the Afrika Korps [German combat units in North Africa] could have been destroyed by a more vigorous exploitation after the breakthrough, but let us remember the realities of the time.

"Monty had his first big command. He was new to the desert. He was fighting a great battlefield tactician in Rommel, whose troops were seasoned warriors: he and they had won some remarkable victories; whereas the Eighth Army had only recently been reformed and given the material to take on the Axis at better odds; many of our fresh reinforcements were new to desert conditions; and although our Intelligence was good we couldn't know accurately what punch the Germans were still nursing."

Harold Alexander, *The Alexander Memoirs: 1940–45* (Cassell, 1962)

invaded Papua New Guinea and now faced a fierce counterattack by the Australian forces, which the Australians finally won in January 1943.

THE FIGHT FOR NORTH AFRICA

As the war raged in the Pacific, German forces pursued land in North Africa, led by Field Marshal Rommel. Like Japan in the Pacific, Germany experienced successes in the first part of 1942. In June, German forces seized Tobruk from the British and advanced into Egypt. But the German and Italian advance was halted by British commander General Sir Claude Auchinleck in July, at the First Battle of El Alamein. Churchill was anxious to destroy the Axis forces in North Africa once and for all and ordered a further attack. He was under pressure from Joseph Stalin, the Soviet leader, to begin an invasion of occupied Europe, but he wanted to complete the African campaign first. Churchill appointed a new general, Bernard Montgomery, to take command of the Eighth Army and win the fight in Egypt.

British general Bernard Montgomery in Egypt during the North African campaign. Montgomery resisted Churchill's demands to launch a renewed attack at El Alamein as quickly as possible. He waited until October, and then launched a successful attack.

A fleet of U.S. ships heads for northwest Africa to join Operation Torch. This was the name given to the Allied invasion of the region in November 1942. At first, U.S. military leaders favored a landing in Europe, but by July 1942 they accepted that this strategy was best.

In October, Montgomery mounted his counterattack against the Axis Powers. His forces outnumbered the Germans and Italians by about two to one. Montgomery achieved victory for the Allies at the Second Battle of El Alamein, although he did not completely destroy Field Marshal Rommel's army.

In November, American and British forces followed this victory with an invasion of northwest Africa. The aim was to defeat German and Italian forces in the Mediterranean. British troops landed in French-controlled Morocco and Algeria. In reply, the Germans occupied southern France and Tunisia, which were also under French control. The Germans and Italians poured troops into Tunisia in December. Now the Axis forces in northwest Africa outnumbered the U.S., British, and French forces. The conflict in the region was not over yet.

NAZI HORROR

Meanwhile in Europe, the Nazis were pursuing a devastating campaign against the Jews. Hitler was determined to get rid of all Jewish people and began a systematic campaign of mass murder that would shock the world. During his rise to power in 1933, Hitler stripped Jewish people of their rights and imprisoned many Jews in concentration camps. In the autumn of 1941, the Nazis began to deport Jews from Germany and German-occupied countries to ghettos in Poland. Hitler organized death squads called Einsatzgruppen (mobile killing units) to round up Jews, Roma people (gypsies), and Communists and kill them. At the end of 1941, the Nazis started to build death camps where they could murder their enemies.

This policy of systematic murder was given a name—the Final Solution—at the Wannsee Conference in January 1942. At this meeting, senior Nazi officials decided to formally adopt a policy of exterminating the entire Jewish population of Europe—an estimated 11 million people. Their plan was to deport all the European Jews to work camps and death camps in Poland. The fittest would be worked to death while the others would be killed immediately. The Germans invested in sophisticated technology to create gas chambers so they could kill thousands of Jews—men, women, and children— daily, using poison gas. This attempt

WHY DID IT HAPPEN ?

Did Hitler plan the Holocaust?

Some historians who have made a special study of the Holocaust, such as Lucy Dawidowicz, believe that Hitler's intention to annihilate the Jews was planned much earlier than the Wannsee Conference in 1942. She argues that Hitler had expressed his hatred of the Jews since 1919 and had always sought to be rid of them.

Other historians, such as Martin Broszat, argue that the policy to destroy the Jews developed as World War II progressed and the Nazis gained greater control over Europe. The Nazis took advantage of the situation created by the war.

Steven R. Welch, *A Survey of Interpretive Paradigms in Holocaust Studies and a Comment on the Dimensions of the Holocaust* (Yale University, 2001)

Children pictured at Auschwitz concentration camp in 1945. They are some of the very few survivors. In camps such as Auschwitz in Poland, inmates were forced to work until they died of exhaustion. There was also a death camp at Auschwitz, called Birkenau, where Jews were deliberately murdered in gas chambers—it is thought that over a million people died in Auschwitz-Birkenau.

A female welder in a German factory producing Messerschmitt aircraft. Workers were transported from occupied countries to work in German munitions factories. At the beginning of the war, volunteers and prisoners were used, but by 1941, the Nazis forced foreign workers to work in their arms factories. The conditions for most foreign workers were appalling.

to wipe out an entire people became known as the Holocaust.

THE SIEGE OF STALINGRAD

In 1942, the Germans mounted a renewed offensive against the USSR. Their aim was to destroy Soviet military and economic power. The first step was to capture Stalingrad and seize the oilfields in the Caucasus to the south. In August, German forces besieged Stalingrad, which was fiercely defended by the Russians. Commander of the most southern Nazi army, General Paul Ludwig von Kleist, led his troops toward the Caucasus, but his army was not prepared for the treacherous deep snowfalls in October, which meant he could advance no further. The Germans never reached the main oilfields.

AIR AND SEA BATTLES

Throughout 1942, Britain and Germany's air forces attacked each other relentlessly; the RAF bombed the German cities of Lübeck, Cologne, and Hamburg, and the Luftwaffe bombed Exeter, Bath, and other English cities. Meanwhile at sea, the Germans had some success in the Battle of the Atlantic. In early 1942, they had changed the Enigma code so the Allies could not discover the whereabouts of German U-boats. The U.S., which had entered the Battle of the Atlantic to support the Allies, had not introduced protective measures against the U-boats, such as traveling in convoys, and lost many surface ships. German U-boats succeeded in sinking nearly 500 Allied ships in the first half of 1942.

CHAPTER 4

THE ALLIES ATTACK

The beginning of 1943 saw the Allies gaining advantages over the Axis Powers as they fought back in battles on land, sea, and in the air. In January 1943, Churchill and Roosevelt held a conference in Casablanca to discuss the progress of the war. They announced that "unconditional surrender" by the Axis Powers was their ultimate aim. At the time, the Soviet Union was under fierce attack by German forces and wanted the Allies to establish a second front against Germany. For example, if the Allies invaded northern France and then went on to attack Germany, this would force Hitler to divide his army and so weaken the offensive against the USSR. But Britain and the U.S. were resistant to the idea of opening up a second front. Despite this, the USSR had some successes against Germany in 1943, as its forces managed to hold out against the Nazis on the Eastern Front. Meanwhile, Japan and Germany suffered defeats in the Far East and North Africa.

The tide of war was also turning at sea. In March, in the Battle of the Atlantic, the Germans lost just one U-boat. However, in April, as a result of improved antisubmarine tactics, better weapons, and new technology, the Allies began to sink more and more U-boats. By May, Germany had lost 41 U-boats and Hitler called off the battle. A total of between 75,000 and 85,000 Allied seamen and about 9,000 U-boat seamen had died during the campaign.

A British soldier searches a German prisoner captured in Tunisia in 1943. When the Axis forces surrendered in May 1943, the Allies took more than 250,000 prisoners, including 125,000 German troops.

DEFEAT IN THE EAST

Germany's war aims were not going well in the east, either: the Axis Powers were losing battles to the USSR. In February 1943, Soviet forces defeated the Germans and their allies—the Romanian, Hungarian, and Italian armies—at the battle of Stalingrad. This was the first major loss of Hitler's armies in the USSR, and it was a huge blow to German morale as well

TURNING POINTS IN HISTORY

Kursk—the battle of the tanks

From the outset, the Soviet forces were in a good position at the Battle of Kursk, with far more guns, soldiers, and better tanks than the Germans. On July 5, the Germans attacked, and a week later the Russians counterattacked. This was the biggest tank battle in history, with 1,500 tanks engaged on each side. The Russians were victorious, putting an end to Hitler's aim of conquering the Soviet Union.

as a decisive military defeat. A more significant battle took place in July when, in the Battle of Kursk, Soviet forces again defeated the Germans. The battles around Kursk cost Hitler half a million men, and it was now apparent that Germany could no longer win the war in the east. Between August and December, the Soviet forces advanced, extending the fighting along a wide front from the Baltic in the north to the Black Sea in the south.

Germany was also suffering heavy losses on other fronts. In March 1943, U.S. and British forces defeated Rommel's army at the Battle of Medenine, in southern Tunisia. Rommel realized the German army was in a weak position and warned Hitler that it was "plain suicide" for the Axis forces to remain in North Africa. By mid-May, the

German soldiers inside a heavily bombed factory in Stalingrad in 1942. The battle for the city of Stalingrad was a major success for the Allies. After several weeks of fighting, Nazi General Friedrich Paulus surrendered on January 31, 1943. The Germans lost 200,000 men at Stalingrad, while 110,000 more were taken prisoner.

December 1942—British forces, Indian troops, and Gurkhas (soldiers from the Nepalese force in the British army) face a Japanese attack from across a river in Burma.

VOICES FROM HISTORY

"Sheer misery..."

The Commander of the 32nd U.S. Army Division, Lieutenant-General R. L. Eichelberger, described the appalling environment soldiers endured fighting on the island of Papua in the Pacific:

"It was about one part fighting to three parts sheer misery of physical environment. It was climbing up one hill and down another, and then, when breath was short, fording streams with weapons held aloft or wading through swamps. It was sweat and then chill; it was a weariness of body and spirit; and once again tropical illness was a greater foe than enemy bullets."

R. L. Eichelberger, *Jungle Road to Tokyo* (Odhams Press, 1951)

Allies had conquered Tunisia, forcing the Axis troops in North Africa to surrender. The Allies were in complete control of the region.

While the North African campaign continued, in the Far East Japan was still in a strong position at the beginning of 1943. The Allies could not reach China because the Japanese were in control of Burma. In December 1942, British forces had launched a land offensive in Burma in an attempt to defeat Japan and reopen the Burma road—the route between India and the temporary capital of China, Chungking. But the Japanese took cover in the mountains and rain forests, both difficult habitats in which to fight, and the British were forced to withdraw in May 1943.

PACIFIC ISLAND BATTLES

Elsewhere, however, Japanese forces were not so successful. In February 1943, Japan lost Guadalcanal and Papua in the Pacific, and could no longer advance southward. As a result, Japan decided to concentrate on the defense of strategic points, especially New Guinea and the Solomon Islands. At a U.S. military conference in March 1943, counterattacks against the Japanese to win back these regions were announced. A key objective was to capture the powerful Japanese naval base at Rabaul, where about 110,000 Japanese troops were based.

The United States forces continued their strategy of island hopping to reconquer territory from Japan. In May, U.S. soldiers recaptured the Aleutian Islands. Then, finally, they attacked the island of Attu, where most of the 2,300 defenders were killed.

Following these successes, in June the Americans began their attack on the Japanese forces in New Georgia and the Solomon Islands. United States general Douglas MacArthur's strategy was to break the lines of communication between the Japanese-held islands and isolate them from each other. Each Japanese-held island was able to communicate with the next island in the chain, but was not able to communicate with more distant Japanese-held islands. This meant that rather than attack a Japanese stronghold head-on, MacArthur would attack the next Japanese-held island in the chain. This broke lines of communication between the islands and isolated them, thus making them easier to conquer.

The Japanese launched a fierce counterattack, but were defeated in New Georgia in August and in the Solomon Islands by October. About

November 1943—U.S. marines wade knee-deep in mud on their way to attack Japanese troops on Bougainville, the largest of the Solomon Islands. This was the last major operation of the Solomons campaign.

10,000 Japanese soldiers were killed defending the Solomon Islands, while the Americans lost 1,150 troops. Allied forces then moved in on the naval garrison on Rabaul. By capturing the islands around Rabaul and building air bases on each island, the Allies effectively isolated Rabaul so that it could not be resupplied. By spring 1944, the base at Rabaul was of no use to the Japanese.

INVADING ITALY
Meanwhile in Europe, the Allies' next objective was to attack the Axis Powers by invading Italy. They decided

U.S. troops leave their landing craft and wade ashore at the start of the invasion of Salerno, Italy, in September 1943. The Allied commanders believed that the landing would be virtually unopposed, but the Germans mobilized six divisions, who fiercely resisted the invasion.

WHY DID IT HAPPEN ?

Why was the second front delayed?

The U.S. Chiefs of Staff had suggested proposals for a major invasion of France in the spring of 1943, but Britain persuaded the Americans to drop the plan. Historian A. J. P. Taylor argued that this was because it would not have been possible for the Allies to open a second front before 1944 because the U.S. and Britain were not ready. In order to launch a successful sea invasion of France, they needed to restore their command of the oceans and build more ships. Also, for such an operation to be successful, careful and lengthy planning was required—it was not something that could be rushed.

In contrast, radical historian Gabriel Kolko argued that Churchill wanted to postpone this second front against Germany for a more indirect strategy that favored Britain in particular—the invasion of North Africa—which would protect British colonial interests in the Mediterranean.

A. J. P. Taylor, *The Second World War* (Hamish Hamilton, 1975); Gabriel Kolko, *The Politics of War* (Pantheon, 1990)

A B-17 Flying Fortress bomber targets an industrial area in Cologne, Germany. When they flew beyond the range of their escort fighter planes, these bombers were vulnerable to attack by German fighters. In December 1943, a long-range fighter, the P-51 Mustang, was introduced to protect B-17 bombers on missions over enemy territory.

to invade the island of Sicily from Tunisia and use this as a base to move northward to occupy the entire country.

The invasion of Italy began in July 1943, when Mussolini's fascist government was already on the edge of economic collapse. Mussolini no longer had the support of the people and at the end of July, King Victor Emanuel dismissed him and appointed General Pietro Badoglio as head of government. In September, Badoglio surrendered to the Allies. But Germany was not prepared to give up control of Italy and sent Nazi forces to counterattack. These forces disarmed the Italian troops in Rome, and the king fled. On the day that Badoglio's surrender was broadcast, the Allies landed in Salerno in southern Italy to face a fierce defense by the Germans under the command of Albert Kesselring. The progress of Allied troops northward was extremely slow and by the end of 1943, the Allies had still not reached Rome.

While German forces were occupied fighting the Allies in Italy and elsewhere, their home country was under attack. In 1943, the Allies intensified their bombing raids on Germany. U.S. B-17 Flying Fortress bombers operated during daylight and British Bomber Command carried out raids by British planes at night. They attacked the Ruhr, Hamburg, and Berlin, with devastating results— thousands of German civilians died and tens of thousands lost their homes. Yet the bombings did not succeed in knocking out weapons factories as the Allies had hoped, so German arms production was hardly affected.

CHAPTER 5

VICTORY IN SIGHT

The Axis Powers had endured many setbacks during 1943, but at the end of the year the German and Japanese empires were still largely intact. Churchill, Roosevelt, and Stalin met in Tehran, Iran, in November 1943 for a conference, where they pledged to work together until Germany was defeated. They decided that the Allies should mount an invasion of northern France by May 1944. This offensive became known as Operation Overlord.

Meanwhile, the Allied campaign in Italy was progressing. In January 1944, Allied forces landed at Anzio, south of Rome. The Germans had established the Gustav Line in the mountains just north of Anzio, and the Allies were determined to break through it to move northward. The Germans put up a strong resistance to the Allied attacks, but in May the Allies succeeded in breaking through the Gustav Line. By the end of the month, German defenses collapsed In June, the U.S. Army marched on the capital, Rome, having won an important tactical and symbolic victory.

THE D-DAY LANDINGS

While fighting continued in Italy, the carefully planned Allied landings in Normandy, northwest France, finally took place. The first day of landings was given the code name D-Day, for the unspecified day on which the military attack would be launched. On June 5, minesweepers cleared a lane

U.S. general Mark Clark and his troops in Rome following the liberation of the city in June 1944. Clark commanded the Allied forces during the Italian campaign. The conquest of Rome was important symbolically to the Allies, even though the Germans soon formed a new defensive line north of the city.

VOICES FROM HISTORY

A German's perspective

The D-Day attacks are described by Franz Gockel, a German soldier whose 18th birthday was on D-Day:

"The opponent wanted to 'defeat' us, as it was called in those days, and we did our best in order to repel this opponent, and we did not think about the individual human being. When the landing troops arrived, we saw that on every single boat there were more soldiers than in our entire bay of six kilometres. ... this large one [landing boat] which landed right in front of us had about 200–300 men, and they had their exit on both sides, and stood bunched up ... and one comrade who was 50 metres in front of me ... came crawling into my bunker, and shouted, 'Franz, beware, they are coming. Now you have to defend yourself.' And this is what we both did."

Quoted on the BBC History website

A U.S. soldier on lookout duty from a foxhole on a beach in Normandy. The Allied Expeditionary Force made the first landings in France on D-Day, June 6, 1944. A sign in German above the soldier warns that there are minefields in the area.

through the English Channel and 5,000 vessels followed. That night, French resistance fighters sabotaged rail and communication links in France in a coordinated move to help support the Allies. Early on June 6, Allied ships fired on German defensive positions in eastern Normandy, and British, Canadian, and U.S. soldiers landed on French soil. Germany fought back and the battles were intense, but within a few weeks the Allies began to push back the Germans and began to make progress eastward through France.

By late 1944, German troops had been cleared from most of France and Belgium. In December, the Allied troops marched through Belgium toward Germany, believing that the war was won. They were taken by surprise when the Germans launched a fierce counterattack at Ardennes in an attempt to prevent an Allied invasion of Germany. This became popularly known as the Battle of the Bulge. The attack, however, was unsuccessful, and in January 1945 the Germans withdrew.

The Allied victory at the Battle of Ardennes brought German defeat ever

The leaders of the most important Allied nations (from left): Churchill, Roosevelt, and Stalin at the Yalta Conference of February 1945.

VOICES FROM HISTORY

Was mass bombing necessary?

The bombing of German cities such as Dresden was authorized by Winston Churchill. However, it seems that he later came to the conclusion that the bombing had been unnecessary, as Germany was already on the point of collapse. On March 28, 1945, Churchill wrote to the Chief of Staffs Committee:

"It seems to me that the moment has come when the question of bombing of German cities simply for the sake of increasing the terror, though under other pretexts, should be reviewed. ... Otherwise we may come into control of an utterly ruined land. ... The destruction of Dresden remains a serious query against the conduct of Allied bombing."

Many British people condemned the mass bombing of Germany as unnecessary. But others, such as Sir Arthur Harris, head of RAF Bomber Command, continued to argue even after the war that it was crucial in helping to bring the conflict to an end. He wrote:

"In spite of all that happened at Hamburg, bombing proved a comparatively humane method. For one thing, it saved the youth of this country and of our allies from being mown down by the military as it was in the war of 1914–1918."

Churchill quoted in *Socialist Review*, UK (February 1995); Sir Arthur Harris, writing in his memoirs, *Bomber Offensive* (Greenhill Books, 1947)

closer. At the start of 1945, the Allies prepared for victory. At the Yalta Conference in February 1945, Roosevelt, Churchill, and Stalin discussed what would happen in Europe after the war, and drew up plans for the establishment of the United Nations.

On January 12, 1945, Stalin launched an offensive against Germany from the east, the start of the Allied strategy to reclaim eastern Europe. The Soviet troops advanced rapidly. They took Warsaw in Poland and by the end of the month were approaching the German capital, Berlin. On January 27, Soviet troops liberated the prisoners in the Auschwitz concentration camp. As they helped the few emaciated survivors, the Allies had their first encounter with the true horrors of Hitler's Holocaust policy.

As the Soviet troops advanced from the east, the Allies renewed their bombing campaign against Germany. British bombers attacked Dresden in February, killing between 25,000 and over 100,000 people. The purpose of this strategy was to force German air power away from other territories to concentrate on the defense of their homeland and to divert German workers away from arms production.

While Soviet forces attacked Germany from the east, the western Allies moved in from the south and west. Soviet troops pushed the Germans out of Budapest, Hungary, in February, out of Czechoslovakia in March, and out of Vienna in April. On April 16, they attacked Berlin and by April 29, Hitler knew he had lost the war. Meanwhile, British, U.S., Canadian, and French forces advanced through Italy, and on April 29, the German forces there surrendered. The following day, Hitler committed suicide in his bunker in the ruins of Berlin, and on May 7, Germany surrendered. May 8, 1945, became known as VE Day, or Victory in Europe Day.

STRUGGLE WITH JAPAN

While Germany was close to defeat, Japan's empire was also pushed back during 1944. Since the Battle of

In April 1945, Soviet and German troops fought on the streets of Berlin as Soviet forces gained control of Germany's capital. Stalin wanted his to be the first Allied troops to reach Berlin and ordered two million Soviet troops to advance on the city.

U.S. Marines land on the beach in Saipan in June 1944. Both the U.S. and Japan amassed large numbers of troops to fight for control of the island. Before the fighting started, the Japanese admiral sent a message to his fleet which said, "The fate of the empire rests on this one battle."

Midway, Japan had suffered serious fuel shortages and could not produce sufficient new ships and aircraft to make up for its losses. Yet despite these problems, in spring 1944, Japanese forces were still extending their control in China, and moved into the interior of the country. The Chinese forces were unable to resist their advance. However, the Allies decided that China was no longer an important area of conflict and instead planned to defeat Japan in other places, such as Burma, Saipan, and the Philippines.

The United States wanted to reopen the Burma road and thought the British should attack the Japanese forces in Burma to achieve this. The Japanese were determined to defend it and attacked first, but their offensive failed and the British advanced into Burma.

Saipan in the Mariana Islands was a vital stronghold in the outer defenses of Japan's empire. If Saipan was taken, Japan's national defenses would no longer be effective because its capture brought Japan within range of U.S. B-29 bombers. In June, the Americans invaded Saipan. The battle was a disaster for Japan, which lost nearly 400 aircraft and thousands of men. The fall of Saipan was a severe setback for the Japanese military and political command. Prime minister General Tojo Hideki resigned over this failure and was replaced by General Koiso Kuniaki.

The end was now in sight for the Japanese. The United States forces swept through the Pacific and captured the strongholds of Tinian and Guam in August. Then, in October, General MacArthur launched an attack on the Philippines, which ended with the conquest of the capital, Manila, in

Was D-Day vital to victory?

Each year on June 6, the countries that fought Germany remember the D-Day landings in Normandy. Some historians, such as Martin Gilbert, believe that failure in Normandy could have allowed Hitler to continue to rule western Europe, particularly if the United States had concentrated on the demands of the Pacific war.

However, military historian Professor Richard Holmes believes that the importance of D-Day is overemphasized. As brave as the fighters were, there were broader reasons for the Allied victory. Without the Allied navies keeping the sea lanes open, the destruction of the Luftwaffe by Allied air forces, and the Soviet victories on the Eastern Front, it is unlikely that the D-Day invasion would have succeeded.

Martin Gilbert, *Turning Points in History: D-Day* (Wiley, 2004); Richard Holmes, "The 'D-Day Dodgers,'" BBC History website, 2004

March 1945.

However, during the battles for the Pacific, the U.S. met strong resistance from Japan. For example, when the Americans attacked Iwo Jima in February and the island of Okinawa at the beginning of April, they met fierce resistance. The battles on Okinawa lasted for almost three months. The Japanese defended their positions using kamikaze forces—volunteer suicide pilots who deliberately crashed their aircraft on the decks of ships. Japan's forces suffered enormous casualties, though; by the time the Americans had conquered Okinawa, over 100,000 Japanese had died.

The remains of the deck of the aircraft carrier USS *Bunker Hill* following an attack by Japanese kamikaze pilots near Okinawa, Japan, in May 1945. This attack left 346 men dead, 43 missing, and 264 wounded. Kamikaze pilots were genuine volunteers, although the U.S. forces found it hard to believe that they had not been conscripted.

CHAPTER 6

END OF THE WAR

Japan was the last of the Axis Powers to capitulate to the Allies. In spring 1945, the country was close to collapse. Many factories could no longer operate because they had no coal or raw materials, and two-thirds of Japanese ships had been sunk. American bombers continued to attack, and in one raid on Tokyo on March 8, 83,000 people were killed. (By comparison, 60,000 British civilians were killed in air attacks during the entire war.)

British forces finally drove the Japanese out of Burma in May 1945. The new Japanese prime minister, Baron Suzuki Kantaro, asked Stalin to help negotiate Japan's surrender, but Stalin thought the Japanese desire for peace was not strong enough and refused. Then, in July, the Allies met at a conference in Potsdam, Germany, and called upon Japan to surrender. Suzuki

An industrial area of Tokyo, flattened after U.S. mass bombing in March 1945. The United States Air Force did not focus on specific targets in Japan, but instead used incendiary bombs that created huge firestorms and caused devastation over a wide area.

VOICES FROM HISTORY

The bid for peace

Toshikazu Kase was a senior
Japanese Foreign Ministry
official who was appalled at the
devastation of his country. He was
pro-British and pro-American, and
after the fall of Saipan, he worked
to make peace with the Allies. In
early 1944, he wrote in his diary:

*"Defeat now stares us stark in the face. There
is only one question left: how can we avert
the chaos attendant upon a disastrous defeat?
The preservation of my fatherland, that is a
paramount [most important] task assigned
to me by fate. The hostile attack is developing
so surprisingly swiftly that it may be that
diplomacy cannot intervene before it is too
late. I must redouble my efforts to expedite
[speed up] the restoration of peace."*

Quoted in Peter Calvocoressi, Guy Wint,
and John Pritchard, *The Penguin History of
the Second World War* (Penguin, 1989)

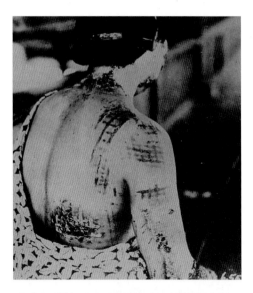

A Japanese woman injured by the explosion
of the atomic bomb in Hiroshima on August
6, 1945. The pattern of the kimono she was
wearing at the time of the explosion is burned
into her skin. Most of the survivors within about
0.3 miles (0.5 km) of the blast died a slow,
painful death from the effects of radiation.

did not give a direct reply, which led
America to think that Japan did not
want to stop fighting, and the war
continued.

HIROSHIMA AND NAGASAKI

Stalin offered to become involved
with the conflict in the Far East, but
American leaders feared this might
give the USSR an opportunity to gain
influence in the region. Instead,
President Harry Truman (who took
office after the death of Roosevelt in
April 1945) decided to use atomic bombs
to force Japan to surrender. Many senior
Americans disagreed with this decision,
including General Dwight Eisenhower,
who had commanded the Allied forces
in Europe. He said later that he believed
"it wasn't necessary to hit them with
that awful thing."

However, the terrible decision had
been made and on August 6, the
Americans dropped the world's first
atomic bomb on the Japanese city
of Hiroshima. Three days later, they
dropped another bomb on the city of
Nagasaki. The effects were devastating.
About 110,000 people died instantly
as the bombs exploded. The two cities
were flattened and atomic radiation
spread over a wide area that led to
thousands more people dying from
dreadful wounds, burns, or leukemia in
the years that followed. On August 14,
Japan agreed to surrender. World War II

41

A group of refugees leaving Lodz, Poland, after its liberation by the USSR. About 60 million people were displaced from their homes during World War II.

was over.

Now the world had to evaluate the cost of the war—and this was enormous. Out of 70 million who fought in the war, over 25 million died, with millions more injured. The Soviet forces lost the largest proportion of their fighters—1 in 22—and the Americans the least— 1 in 500. The civilian death toll was higher: up to 20 million in the USSR and an estimated 4.5 million in Germany. Civilians died in air raids, from forced labor or starvation under siege, or they were deliberately murdered by the Nazis. Poland lost about 20 percent of its population, the USSR 10 percent. Japanese casualties were about 2 million, while deaths in

China numbered somewhere between 2.5 and 13.5 million. The Nazis murdered about 6 million of Europe's 9 million Jews and virtually wiped out the Roma people of eastern Europe.

Many countries were ravaged by the war. Soviet Russia suffered the greatest loss: 1,710 towns and 70,000 villages were destroyed. Vast areas of land were laid to waste, left completely bare and uninhabited. Germany was also war-torn. The city of Hamburg alone suffered more damage than all of Britain. Most Japanese cities lay in ruins. The industrial resources of Poland and France were cut in half. In Britain, 500,000 homes were destroyed.

PEACE AT LAST
At the Potsdam Conference in July and August 1945, the Allies discussed peace, but no agreement was reached until the

VOICES FROM HISTORY

The United Nations

In October 1945, the United States, Britain, and the USSR led the way in drawing up the United Nations charter. The United Nations was to be an international organization that would aim to preserve world peace. This is a summary of its aims:

We the peoples of the United Nations [are] determined to save succeeding generations from the scourge of war, which twice in our lifetime has brought untold sorrow to mankind, and to reaffirm faith in fundamental human rights, in the dignity and worth of the human person, in the equal rights of men and women and of nations large and small, and to establish conditions under which justice and respect for the obligations arising from treaties and other sources of international law can be maintained, and to promote social progress and better standards of life in larger freedom...

Preamble to the UN Charter, June 1945

following year. The Allies finally signed peace treaties with Bulgaria, Finland, Hungary, Italy, and Romania in 1947. It was decided that France, Britain, the USSR, and the U.S. would share control of Germany, and that each power would take reparations from the zone it controlled. The Soviet zone became the Communist state of East Germany in 1949, while the Western Allies merged their zones into the Federal Republic of Germany. The Americans finally made peace with Japan in 1952.

After the war had ended, the United States, Britain, France, and the USSR wanted those responsible punished. They established an International Tribunal and brought alleged war criminals to trial. At the Nuremberg

A street sign separates the American and Soviet zones of Berlin. In 1945, the division of Germany put Berlin within East Germany under Communist rule. However, the city itself was divided into two sections: West Berlin, which was part of the Federal Republic of Germany, and East Berlin, which became the capital of East Germany.

YOU ARE LEAVING
THE AMERICAN SECTOR

ВЫ ВЫЕЗЖАЕТЕ ИЗ
АМЕРИКАНСКОЙ ЗОНЫ

VOUS SORTEZ
DU SECTEUR AMÉRICAIN

IE VERLASSEN DEN AMERIKANISCHEN SEKTOR

Former Japanese prime minister Tojo Hideki testifies in his own defense at the International Tribunal for Far East war crimes in Tokyo in 1947. As a result of the trial, he was convicted and executed.

Trials of 1945–46, twenty-one German leaders were charged with war crimes and eleven were given the death sentence. In a similar trial in Japan, twenty-five leaders were sentenced, of whom eleven were hanged.

A NEW POLITICAL LANDSCAPE

Inevitably, the aftermath of the war brought about far-reaching political changes. In the Far East, the British and the French regained their colonies, albeit temporarily—many Asian countries gained their independence

WHY DID IT HAPPEN

Were the atomic bombs necessary?

In the aftermath of the Hiroshima and Nagasaki bombings, the official U.S. view was that it was necessary to drop the bombs to avoid a lengthy conflict that would have cost the Allies a million casualties. Many historians today agree with this analysis.

However, J. Samuel Walker, chief historian of the U.S. Nuclear Regulatory Commission, reviewed the recent research in 1990: "Careful scholarly treatment of the records and manuscripts opened over the past few years has greatly enhanced our understanding of why the Truman administration used atomic weapons against Japan. Experts continue to disagree on some issues, but critical questions have been answered. The consensus among scholars is that the bomb was not needed to avoid an invasion of Japan and to end the war within a relatively short time. It is clear that alternatives to the bomb existed and that Truman and his advisers knew it." Many military specialists today argue that Japan would have surrendered without either an invasion or the dropping of atomic bombs.

J. Samuel Walker, "The Decision to Use the Bomb: A Historiographical Update," *Diplomatic History 14* (Winter 1990)

after 1945. The United States was given trusteeship over important strategic islands in the Pacific. The Japanese empire was broken up and a new political system created that did not permit the development of military power. The Western powers withdrew from China, and in 1949 it became a Communist state.

The biggest political development was the creation of two new world superpowers: the USSR and the United States. From 1945, the USSR set up Communist governments in the eastern European countries it had conquered during the final phase of the war. The United States, which had provided financial backing for its allies during the war, had become the strongest country economically and now exerted worldwide influence.

The communist USSR and the democratic U.S. now became enemies. In March 1946, Winston Churchill said in a speech in Fulton, Missouri: "From Stettin in the Baltic, to Trieste, in the Adriatic, an iron curtain has descended across the [European] continent. Behind that curtain...all are subject to Soviet influence and a very high degree of control from Moscow [the Soviet capital]." This speech is generally said to mark the start of the Cold War, a struggle for global power and influence between the ideologically opposed Soviet Union and United States. In March 1947, Truman declared that the United States would support other countries against Communist invasion. The world became divided once again—this time between the Communists and the U.S. and its allies—a division that was to last for nearly half a century.

Russian and American troops at the Elbe River in Torgau, Germany, discuss military plans during the final stages of the Allied invasion of Germany in April 1945. Although they were Allies during the war, once peace was established their political differences meant that their cooperation was short-lived.

WORLD WAR II TIMELINE

1937 War breaks out between China and Japan

1938

March 12: Hitler incorporates Austria into Germany

September 29: The Munich Agreement: Czechoslovakia cedes land to Germany, Hungary, and Poland

1939

March 15: Nazi forces occupy all of Czechoslovakia

May 22: Hitler and Mussolini form an alliance, the Pact of Steel

August 23: Nazi-Soviet Nonaggression Pact between Germany and the USSR

September 1: Hitler invades Poland; Britain and France declare war

1940

April 9: Germany invades Denmark and Norway

May 10: Germany invades the Netherlands, Belgium, Luxembourg, and France

June 10: Mussolini declares war on the Allies

June: The Battle of the Atlantic starts

July–October: The Battle of Britain

August 3: Italian forces advance into British Somaliland

August 23: The Blitz begins

September 27: Tripartite Pact between Japan, Italy, and Germany

1941

March 24: Rommel's forces mount first attacks in North Africa

June 22: Germany invades the USSR

December 7: Japan attacks the U.S. at Pearl Harbor. The U.S. and Britain declare war on Japan; Germany and Italy declare war on the U.S.

December 8: Japan starts invasions of southeast Asian countries

1942

June 4–7: Battle of Midway

June 21: Germans take Tobruk and advance into Egypt

October 23: Start of Second Battle of El Alamein

November 8: Allies begin invasion of northwest Africa

1943

February 7: U.S. forces complete the defeat of the Japanese at Guadalcanal

May 13: The Germans surrender in North Africa

June 20: U.S. forces land on New Georgia

July 5–12: Soviet forces defeat the Germans at the Battle of Kursk, Russia

July 10: Allies invade Sicily

November 2: U.S. conquers the Solomon Islands

1944

January 22: Allied forces land in Anzio, Italy

June 6: Allied D-Day landings in northern France

July 9: Fall of Saipan (Mariana Islands) to the U.S.

August 24: Liberation of Paris by Allied troops

1945

January 16: Allies defeat Germans in the Ardennes

January: Soviet forces advance toward Germany

February 28: U.S. forces conquer Manila, capital of the Philippines

April 1: U.S. troops land on Okinawa

April 28: Mussolini is killed by Italian partisans

April 29: German forces capitulate in Italy

April 30: Hitler commits suicide in his Berlin bunker

May 2: German troops surrender in Berlin

May 3: British capture Rangoon, Burma from the Japanese

May 4: Germany surrenders

August 6 and 9: U.S. drops atomic bombs on Hiroshima and Nagasaki

September 2: Japan surrenders

GLOSSARY

appeasement The policy of offering concessions to an aggressor in an attempt to prevent conflict.

atomic bomb A nuclear weapon with violent explosive power that destroys everything in the range of the explosion and releases radiation into the atmosphere.

collaborate To cooperate with or willingly assist.

Communist Someone who believes in communism, a political system in which the state's property is owned by the people and where the country's wealth is shared equally amongst all workers.

concentration camp A prison camp set up by the Nazis for the detention of political prisoners and people that they saw as enemies, especially the Jews. Prisoners were often worked to death but not deliberately murdered.

conscription Compulsory military service.

convoy A group of ships traveling together with military protection.

coup A violent or illegal seizure of power.

death camps Camps in Poland where Jews and other minority groups were taken to be killed.

embargo An order by a state to stop trade.

ghetto An enclosed and guarded area of a town or city where Jews under Nazi occupation were forced to live.

reparations Compensation for war damage that is paid by the defeated state to the victors.

resistance General term for the underground movements formed in Europe to resist the Nazi occupation.

Roma A traditionally nomadic people originally from India, who mostly lived in Europe.

sabotage Deliberate damage to production or transport.

sanctions Military or economic action by a state to try to force another to comply with its wishes or with an international agreement.

tribunal A court of justice.

trusteeship Supervisory control by a country over a territory.

FURTHER INFORMATION

Books:

Adams, Simon. *World War II*. New York: DK Publishing, 2004.

Gavin, Philip. *World War II: Europe*. Farmington Hills, MI: Lucent Books, 2004.

Goldstein, Margaret. *World War II: Europe*. Minneapolis, MN: Lerner Publications, 2004.

Grant, Reg. *World War II*. New York: DK Publishing, 2008.

Hatt, Christine. *Documenting History: World War II: 1939–45*. London: Franklin Watts, 2001.

Nardo, Don. *World War II*. Farmington Hills, MI: Greenhaven Press, 2005.

Sheehan, Sean. *World War II: The Pacific*. London: Franklin Watts, 2004.

Web Sites:

The History Place: World War II in Europe (http://www.historyplace.com/worldwar2/timeline/ww2time.htm)

The Perilous Fight: America's World War II in Color (http://www.pbs.org/perilousfight/)

World War 2: 1939–1945 (http://www.worldwar-2.net/)

Publisher's note to educators and parents: Our editors have carefully reviewed these Web sites to ensure that they are suitable for students. Many Web sites change frequently, however, and we cannot guarantee that a site's future contents will continue to meet our high standards of quality and educational value. Be advised that students should be closely supervised whenever they access the Internet.

INDEX

Numbers in **bold** refer to pictures